There's No Time for Love,

Charlie Brown

Charles M. Schulz

Random House • New York

Library of Congress Cataloging in Publication Data
Schulz, Charles M   There's no time for love, Charlie Brown   I.   Title.   PN6728.P4S33
741.5'973   74-16483   ISBN 0-394-83048-2   ISBN 0-394-93048-7 (lib. bdg.)
Manufactured in the United States of America   1 2 3 4 5 6 7 8 9 0

ABCDEFGHIJK   890   R

You're really something, Sally. Do you know that?

I've never seen anyone who was so uptight about school. Why don't you just relax?

Who can relax?

I'm very discouraged, Chuck.

You know we still have three months of school left.

Tests to take, reports to write . . . all those dumb things to do!

There's no time for love, Chuck!

I got a C in history, Linus.

I got a C in math. I got a C in English and I got a C in reading.
. . . I got a C in everything.

I'm a straight "blah" student.

We're going to have to learn the metric system, Franklin. By the time we grow up, the metric system will probably be official.

One inch is 2.54 centimeters. One foot is 0.3048 meters, and one mile is 1.609 kilometers.

I'll never measure anything again as long as I live.

I wonder if I'll be beautiful when I'm a senior in high school, Chuck. If I knew I wasn't going to be beautiful, I wouldn't bother having graduation pictures taken.

Chuck, would you want my graduation picture sitting on your piano?

We don't have a piano, Peppermint Patty.

That's what I like about you, Chuck. You're always right there with a quick wishy-washy answer!

Lucy, just listen to this problem.

A man has a daughter and a son. The son is three years older than the daughter. In one year the man will be six times as old as the daughter is now, and in 10 years he will be 14 years older than the combined ages of his children. What is the man's present age?

I'm sorry, sir, we are unable to complete your call. . . . Please check the number and dial again.

What's wrong, Charlie Brown?

I just got terrible news, Linus. The teacher says we're going on a field trip to an art museum . . . and I have to get an A on my report or I'll fail the whole course.

Why do we have to have all this pressure about grades, Linus?

Sir, I just heard that we have to go on a field trip. I'm scared to death of field trips.

Marcie, a field trip is lots of fun. You'll like it!

But what if I get sick? What if I get lost? I hear you have to bring your lunch on a field trip....What about that, sir? What if I get out there and discover that I left my lunch on the bus?

What if I get on the wrong bus and end up downtown or something?

Don't worry, Marcie. They use the buddy system on field trips, and they always pair off an older student with a younger one.

I guarantee that I'll be your buddy.

Just to make it easier, Marcie, why don't you come over to my house tomorrow morning and we'll walk to school together. You'll see. Everything will be all right.

I appreciate that, sir.

And stop calling me "sir."

Oh, my gosh! I must have overslept.

I don't want to keep Peppermint Patty waiting. After all, I promised her I wouldn't be late.

Good morning, sir. Here I am. . . .
Am I on time?

Good grief! Marcie, it's four
o'clock in the morning.

Go home and come back later!

It's no use. I can't go home now. Couldn't I just stay here, sir?

You might as well. I certainly can't sleep any more.... And stop calling me "sir"!

I don't know why we have to go on a field trip! Why can't we stay in school?

Do you know what going on a field trip means, Charlie Brown?

It means we ride about ten thousand miles on a bus, and we all get sick.

So here I am on a school bus with the whole class going on a field trip.

I should have brought some pills, Snoopy. I'll probably get sick. . . . I should have stayed home. That's what *I* should have done.

Rats! Here we are. Now we'll have to line up! Someday they'll have a field trip where nobody lines up.

You'd better wake up, sir. I think we've arrived.

Come on, Marcie. The kids are already starting to line up.

Snoopy! . . . There's my old buddy Snoopy. Hi, ol' buddy. How are you?

Hey, Chuck! This is a surprise. I didn't know your school was on this field trip, too.

Yeah, we're supposed to give a report on this museum trip and I may fail my whole term.

I know what you mean, Chuck ol' boy. We gotta write an essay on our field trip, too.

I bet you're kinda glad to see me, huh, Chuck? Maybe you could come over to my house tonight and we'll work on our essays together.

I'm glad we're going to do this together, Chuck. Marcie here is scared to death of field trips.

You and I can kinda show her the ropes.

Hey, everybody's left. C'mon. We better catch up with the rest of the kids.

Which building do you think they went into, Chuck?

I guess the art museum must be the one on the right. It's the closest.

This is terrible, Peppermint Patty. It looks like the museum is selling off part of its collection. They're practically giving the stuff away.

These pieces of sculpture look like
stacks of tomato cans in a supermarket.

What's the matter with
you, Marcie? Don't you know
pop art when you see it?

Look at all the paintings, Lucy.

They don't move. I'm not used to looking at pictures that don't move or have commercials.

Maybe we'll see the Ramona Lisa. Try not to have a good time, Linus. This is supposed to be educational.

I have a whole roll of film to shoot. I think I'll turn in an illustrated report.

I can't understand it, Linus. Charlie Brown must be around here someplace.

I saw him outside talking to Peppermint Patty and some kids from the other school.

It's no use, Charlie Brown. I can't look at another exhibit. I can hardly keep my eyes open. That stupid Marcie woke me up at four o'clock this morning.

I hope my being a little tired doesn't offend you, Chuck.

No, not at all. Maybe we should rest for a while before we look at the rest of the exhibits.

That's nice of you, Chuck. You kinda like me, don't you, Chuck?

I'm glad you don't come right out and say it, though. I respect you for that.

That's all I need . . . respect.

Sir, are you all right?

I guess so. . . . Say . . . where's Chuck? He was sitting right here beside me when I fell asleep. We'd better look for him.

You're in love with Chuck, aren't you, sir?

Me?... In love with Chuck?...

How could anyone be in love with boring, dull, wishy-washy old Chuck?

I thought I heard someone sigh, sir.

There he is, Marcie! There's Chuck! Where's he going?

Hey, Chuck, what's the matter? You aren't going home, are you?

I'll bet he heard what you said about him, sir . . . about how he's dull and wishy-washy and . . .

Chuck! Come back! I didn't mean it! I didn't know you were listening, Chuck!!!

Hey, Chuck, wait! I didn't mean it, Chuck. . . .

I want to be friends. . . . I like you.

He's gone, sir. You kind of like him, don't you, sir?

Marcie, stop calling me "sir"!

I want you to know that I enjoyed the field trip, sir. . . . Even though the museum did look a lot like the grocery store in our neighborhood, it was very educational.

I did a bad thing, Marcie. I hurt Chuck's feelings. I just didn't realize he had fallen for me.

Maybe I can think of something that might help, sir.

You can stop calling me "sir"!

Hello? . . .

Hi, Chuck. This is Peppermint Patty, your museum buddy. . . .

Oh, good grief!

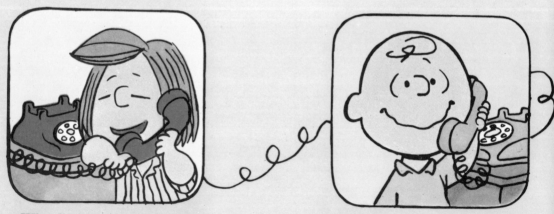

Why don't you come over, and we can write our reports together. Maybe we'll even get an A.

You mean I might not fail, after all?

Hand me the eraser, will you, Chuck?

You touched my hand, Chuck.

You kind of like Chuck, don't you, sir?

Well, good night, Chuck. Good night, Marcie. . . . I think we wrote great reports. We'll probably all get A's.

That was nice of you to help us with the field trip report, Chuck. And thanks for walking me home. Good night. . . .

If you don't want that to be from me, Chuck, think of it as being a good night kiss from Peppermint Patty. She really likes you, you know. All that stuff about "boring, dull, wishy-washy" was just a slip of the tongue.

Hello? Peppermint Patty?

Hello? Oh, is that you,Chuck?

It's kind of embarrassing to say, but I just want to thank you for the good night kiss.

What good night kiss? ! !

That Chuck. He's finally flipped.

I got my slides back from the field trip, Charlie Brown. I'd like your reaction to them.

That's very good, Linus. Your photographs are exactly like the original paintings.

Paintings? I don't remember any paintings like these, Lucy.

I don't remember any of this. I suddenly have the feeling I was in the wrong place!

I handed in my report on our field trip to the museum, Peppermint Patty, but now I realize I wasn't there at all. Marcie was right. We were in a supermarket.

My teacher warned me that only a good grade on my report would save me. . . .

I wrote a report about a trip to a grocery store! . . . I'm doomed!

She's going to hand back our papers, Linus, and I'm going to fail, and I'll get bawled out and I'll probably get kicked out of school, and I'll be disgraced, and I'll spend the rest of my life being a nothing. Why can't I ever do anything right?

. . . Yes, ma'am?

I got an A! I got an A! Look what she wrote on my paper, Linus.

"Your analogy was delightful. Comparing the museum to a supermarket was a stroke of genius."

You know what? You got the only A in the whole class, Charlie Brown.

Chuck, I want to apologize for saying that you're stupid and wishy-washy and everything. It's not easy for a girl to talk like this to a boy, you know. . . .

I know. I always used to think how nice it would be if that little red-haired girl would just come up to me and . . .

I can't stand you, Chuck!

Well, sir, you said the wrong thing again, didn't you?

Kid, I want to ask you something. How come you're always calling me "sir" when I keep asking you not to, huh?

Don't you know how annoying that can be?

No, ma'am.